Christmas CRAFTS

Written by Susannah Bradley

Illustrated by Cathy Hughes

© 1991 Henderson Publishing Limited

Henderson Publishing
Woodbridge, England

Little square 'tree-dec' cards

These are only little, but they are a card and a pressie in one! What the person gets is a card with a tree decoration on it, and when the decoration is taken off and hung on the tree, the card doesn't look as if there's something missing!

1. Our cards were 80 mm square, so for each one we had to cut a piece of card which measured 160 mm × 80 mm, and fold it in half.

2. Start with our star or Christmas box if you like, or think up your own idea. By the time you've made one or two, you'll have had another idea of your own, no doubt!

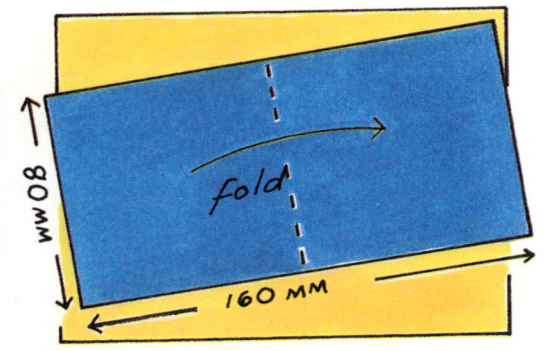

3. You'll see that the idea is a little different for each one. The Christmas Box card has exactly the same picture underneath it so that when you remove the tree decoration the same picture remains. The star is not quite like that — lots of tiny stars in a night sky are there when the big one is taken away.

4. Our decorations were cut out of thick card, but yours could be made of the kind of corrugated card which cardboard boxes are made of. There is a kind of foam-padded board around sometimes which is quite easy to cut with a craft knife, although you should always get an adult to do any craft-knife work for you. It isn't cheating — it's just using the grown-up as an extra hand! And it's much safer than doing it yourself. Polystyrene trays used to package food in the supermarket are good too, and cut well using scissors.

5. Draw the design so that it fills most of the area of your 80 mm square and cut it out. Paint it, or cover it with silver foil or gift wrap.

6. Paint the card. Write HAPPY CHRISTMAS! inside.

7. Make a small hole in the top of the decoration and thread something through for hanging it up. Push this through a small hole in the front of the card and secure with tape at the back.

8. Give yourself a trade name. We put 'This is a Christmas Tree Decoration Card by Bradley Publications' in a box on the back of ours, because Bradley is the surname of the person who wrote this book and of her children who helped her. The other one says 'A Tree-Dec Card by Bob and Jo', not because we know anyone with those names but because they just happened to be the first names we thought of. You could put your own there instead. The trade-name this time is 'Tree-Dec Card' instead of 'Bradley Publications'. It doesn't mean anything, but it is an extra bit of fun.

9. Now then, have you had any bright ideas yet? How about a Christmas pudding? Or a snowman? (Made of white polystyrene you wouldn't have much painting to do). Try to have a light background against a dark decoration, and vice-versa.

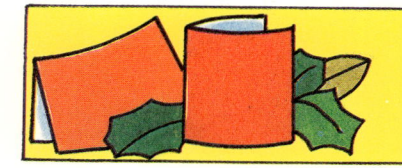

Zig zag cards

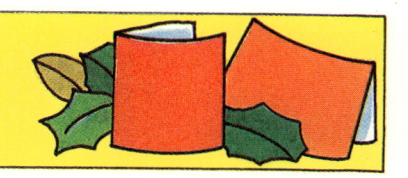

These cards can be made to any measurement you like, but it's best to work it out so that it folds up to fit in an envelope first — or make one yourself (you can find out how on another page in this book).

1. It doesn't matter how wide it is, but **a** and **b** should be the same, and **c** and **d** should be the same as each other, too, but wider than **a** and **b**.

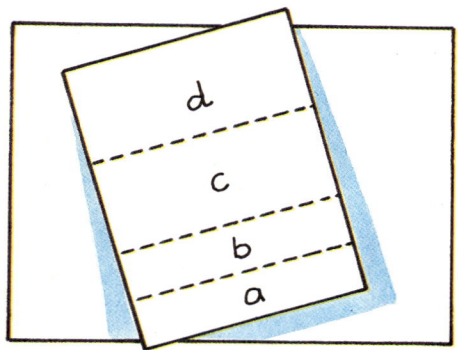

2. Plan your design. Although ours is a rooftop one with Father Christmas, you don't have to copy it. It's nice if you like it enough to want to, but a craft book like this shouldn't just give you one thing, it should make you think up others like it all by yourself.

3. It could be a Christmas tree, with presents stacked up in front of it.
It could be the words MERRY XMAS (to write CHRISTMAS in full would take up too much space).
It could be some angels in the sky, with sheep and shepherds in front, like the bit in the Christmas story where the shepherds heard angels telling them that Jesus had been born.

4. Can you think of anything else? While you are thinking about it, try making one of these. Mark out your card so that the folded card looks like this:

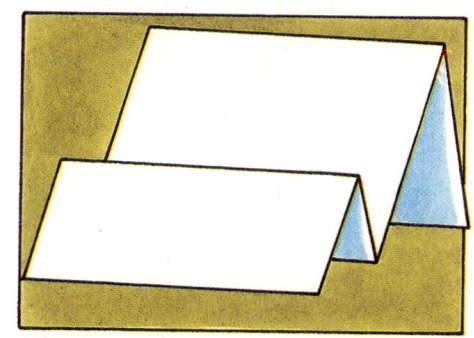

5. Then open it out again.

6. Now draw your picture. The bits which are to stick up are drawn on **b** and **d**. When you have drawn them you snip around the outline you have drawn, where the thick black line is on our diagram.

7. Fold up the snipped shapes so that when you fold the card into the zig-zag again, these pieces stay upright.

8. Draw in the details and colour all the card except the remaining fold-back part of **d**. You can write the message here.

9. This is a special card and will have to be treated like one by the person who gets it, because it isn't the sort you can pin up on the wall.

Card hangers

At Christmas-time everything which is red seems to go up in price if you can find anything left of it in the shops. Fortunately you can usually find crepe paper. You'll need some for this, but you can use a roll of lining paper from the DIY shop and paint it red if you can't get crepe paper. Dark green looks good, too, because it reminds people of fir trees and holly leaves. You'll also need some of that sticky blue stuff which fixes paper to walls.

1. Cut your paper into strips about 50 mm wide, as long as you can fit on your wall, starting about 150 mm below the ceiling. Fix to the wall at the top with the blue sticky stuff. Make a bow out of the paper to fix on the top.

2. When you get some Christmas cards sent to you, fix them down the strip either with staples or more blue sticky stuff. If you use staples, just staple the backs. Then you can look inside as well as at the picture on the front, and you can use the fronts afterwards.

Bows

Adding a bow for a finishing touch can make a present look really special — so here is how to do it. If you've ever got in a muddle with that gift ribbon which sticks to itself when licked, don't despair — next time you try it will be much easier!

You'll need:
Self-adhesive gift ribbon
Scissors
Stapler

1. Cut four pieces of gift ribbon — one which measures 200 mm, one 275 mm, one 350 mm and one 425 mm.

2. Twist the largest piece into a figure of eight shape and dampen to secure it at the ends. Do the same with the next biggest. Place it on top of the first one. Do the same with the other two in turn, and pile them all together in an attractive way. Staple them through the middle — and there is your bow, ready to be put on to a parcel.

Christmas banner

This can be as big as you like — as long as you've got card big enough and tinsel long enough! It's not meant to hang in the middle of a room because the letters look peculiar from the wrong side — hang it against a wall for everyone to get the message.

You'll need:
Coloured card or thick paper (colour it yourself if necessary)
Long piece of tinsel
Sticky blue stuff to hang it up with
Pencil
Scissors

1. Draw out the letters you need, making them all the same size and leaving 30 mm spare card above each one.

2. Cut out the letters, with a tab at each piece which reaches the top of the design (**H** has two tabs but **A** has only one).

3. Fix the tinsel to the wall with sticky blue stuff. Fold the tabs back on each letter and fasten them over the tinsel in the right order with even more sticky blue stuff.

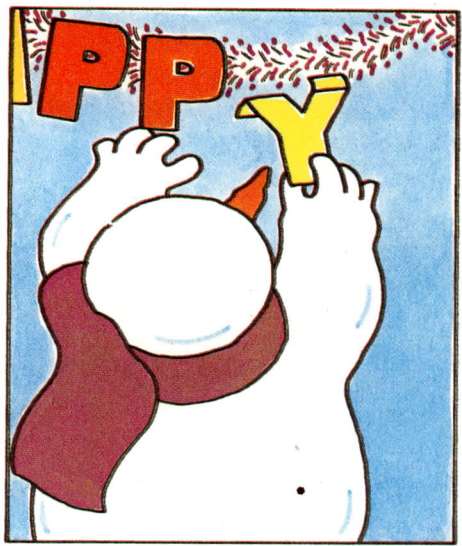

Christmas wreath coasters

Here's a good idea for placing around the house for people to put their drinks on. It'll save Mum and Dad getting cross at finding sticky rings on the furniture on Boxing Day — and they will brighten up the place, too.

You'll need:
Polystyrene trays from the supermarket, the sort you get meat on
Scissors
Pencil
Acrylic paints — red and green
Brushes

1. Draw a Christmas wreath like ours in pencil on to the polystyrene.

2. Cut it out with scissors.

3. Paint leaves in green, and a big red bow and lots of little red berries. Mark the outline of the bow in green and red mixed, making brown.

4. Place them around the house when party time starts.

Pantomime pictures

Christmas is Pantomime time — but whether you're going to one or not, you can have plenty of fun making a special card for someone with a pantomime scene in it.

You'll need:
A clean, empty rectangular cheese box of the kind which has a transparent lid — paint over the writing on the sides
White card and paper
Pencil
Colouring things
Scissors
Transparent sticky tape
Sticky blue stuff used to stick paper to walls

Decide which pantomime you're going to show. We've done 'Little Red Riding Hood'.

1. Cut a piece of paper to fit the inside back of the box and draw a backdrop for your scene. Ours is the woodland scene. Colour it. Fix it in place with tiny bits of sticky blue stuff.

2. Make scenery to fit — you'll need one piece for each side. Colour it and fix it in from the sides with sticky blue stuff. Make your characters. Draw a stand for each one, to make the bases strong enough to stand up. Fix them in place with a blob of sticky blue stuff behind each one. Replace the lid.

3. Cut a front from card, if you like, saying Merry Christmas, and sign your name. Join this to the front with transparent sticky tape. Or, if you'd rather, write a message on card and stick it to the back of the box.

4. You'll find that the whole thing will stand up quite well, at a slightly sloping angle which is ideal for showing off your pantomime scene.

Christmas wreaths

Those Christmas wreaths which you see on people's front doors are really expensive to buy — but you can easily make your own. If you want to make one like you see in the florist's shop, you'll need some gardening wire and fresh greenery, but if you haven't got those, try one of the other kinds we tell you about on this page.

Traditional Front Door Wreath

You'll need:
A wire coat-hanger
Gardening wire
Pine cones
Plenty of evergreen greenery
Red or tartan ribbon
Gold spray paint

1. Spray the cones gold, being careful not to get the spray on anything else (use newspaper and do not do this activity in the best room). Leave to dry.

2. Meanwhile, bend the coat-hanger into a round shape. Bind greenery to it with gardening wire. Start at the top and work down in opposite directions so that the sprigs meet at the bottom.

3. Weave more greenery in amid the first layer, wiring it as you go. It should be nice and firm, with fronds of greenery covering the wire. It is nice to have holly and ivy as well as sprays of bay and cypress.

4. Twist some wire round the cones and fix them into the wreath in three or four places.

5. Tie the ribbon into a big bow and attach with wire either to the top or bottom of the wreath.

Cardboard Wreath

You'll need:
Cardboard boxes
White emulsion paint
Poster or acrylic paints
Polyurethane varnish
White spirit
Brushes
Scissors
Glue
Sticky blue stuff for putting things on walls

1. Draw a circle on card by pencilling round a dinner plate. Remove the dinner plate, put a tea-plate inside the space and draw a smaller circle in the same way, centrally placed within the first one.

2. Cut out the big circle, then cut the centre out so that you have a ring.

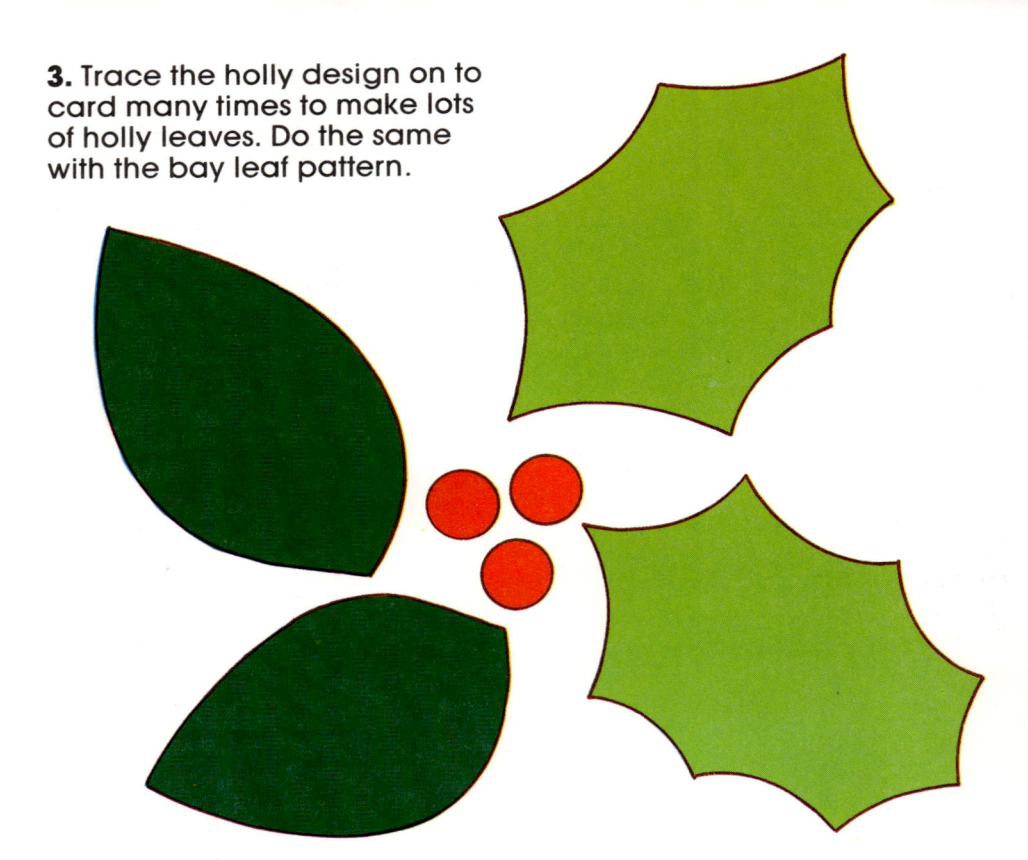

3. Trace the holly design on to card many times to make lots of holly leaves. Do the same with the bay leaf pattern.

4. Cover the ring with holly and bay leaves, glueing them in place. Cut out some more and glue them on top of the first layer.

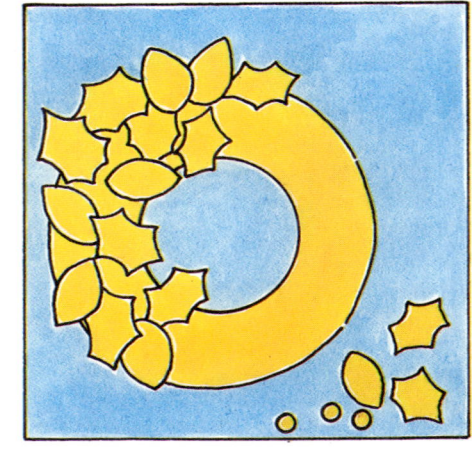

5. Paint the whole thing with white emulsion paint. Wash out the brushes in water, using washing-up liquid.

6. Paint the bay leaves in dark green and the holly leaves in a lighter shade. Add highlights in very pale green, almost white. Paint on red holly berries — or thread some round red beads on to it if you can get any, using gardening wire.

7. When the paint is dry, give the whole thing a coat of polyurethane varnish, placing newspaper underneath to catch drips. Clean the brush you use for this in white spirit, then in warm soapy water.

Fabric Wreath

You'll need:
3 strips of contrasting fabrics in Christmassy colours or patterns, each measuring 10 mm × 1 metre long
Terylene wadding
Needle and thread
Scissors
Wide ribbon in one of the main colours

1. Fold the strips in half lengthways, right sides together, and machine-stitch all down the long edge, taking 5 mm seam allowance. Push through to right side with a knitting pin, pushing terylene wadding into tube as you do so.

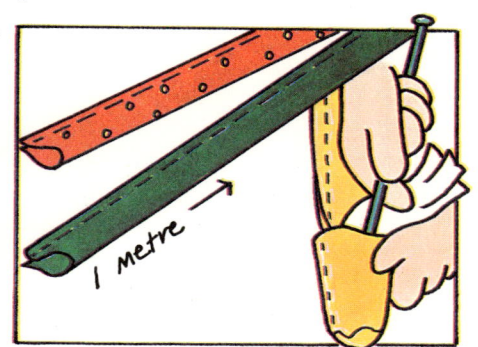

2. When you have three fat tubes, sew all three together at one end, neatening the edges, and then plait them together, pulling tight as necessary to get the plait to form a circle. Join the ends to the starting point, sewing to the underside, and cover the join with a bow made from ribbon. Then it just needs a fabric loop to hang it up.

3. The plaiting needs to be quite tight for this, as it will otherwise not keep its shape. There is no exact size for this as it depends a lot on your plaiting, so you can cut the ends shorter if you find it works better that way.

Christmas bangles

These make good presents — especially as, when Christmas is over, they can be changed back into ordinary bangles again.

You'll need:
Cheap plastic bangles
Christmassy fabric
Glue

1. The fabric you use can be plain if you like, in bright red or green — and if you like you can add tiny bells from a craft shop.

2. Cut a strip of fabric 25 mm wide. Turn and press 5 mm to the wrong side along one long edge.

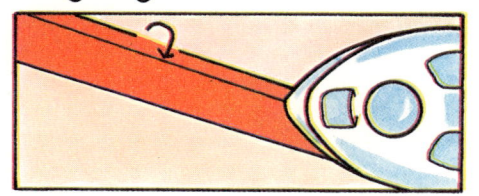

3. Wrap the fabric round and round over the bangle, covering the raw edge with the folded one as you work. When you get back to the starting point, turn in the raw edge and fix in place with glue.

4. Sew a few bells around if you like.

Angels above the manger

This is a mobile to hang up at Christmas. It's quite big and everyone will think you're really clever to have made it when they see it hanging up!

You'll need:
For the angels:
9 sheets of A4 paper
Old tights
Terylene wadding
9 small elastic bands
Transparent sticky tape
Felt pens
Yellow wool
Scissors
Needle and thread

For the manger:
Brown cardboard
Felt pens
Straw
Very small piece of old tights and terylene wadding
Scrap of white cloth

For the main structure:
Wooden coat hanger
Cardboard
Silver foil
Thread
Transparent sticky tape

To make an Angel

1. Fold a sheet of A4 paper in half, then in half again.

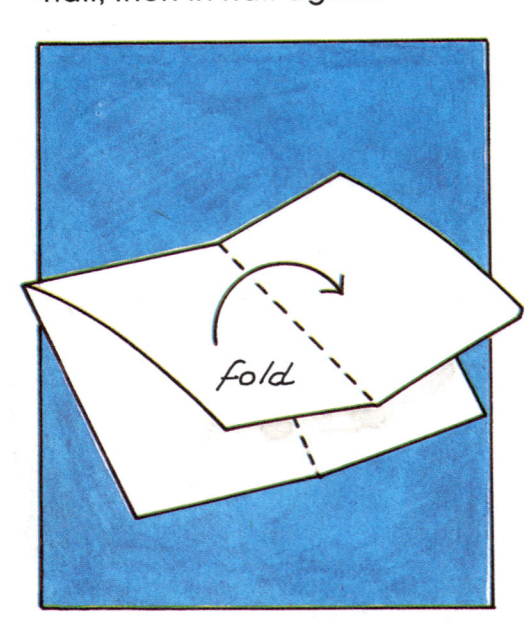

2. Fold again so that one short and one long side are together, with a crease from the corner where these two edges meet.

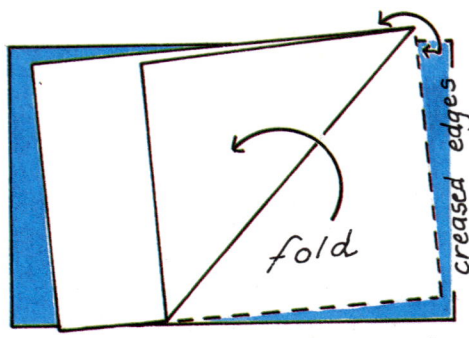

3. Fold in this way again and cut as shown in the diagram.

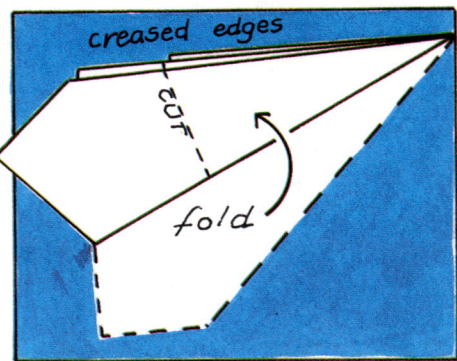

4. Snip triangles out of the sides of the folded paper as shown. Also snip off the very point where the folds meet, to make a small central hole.

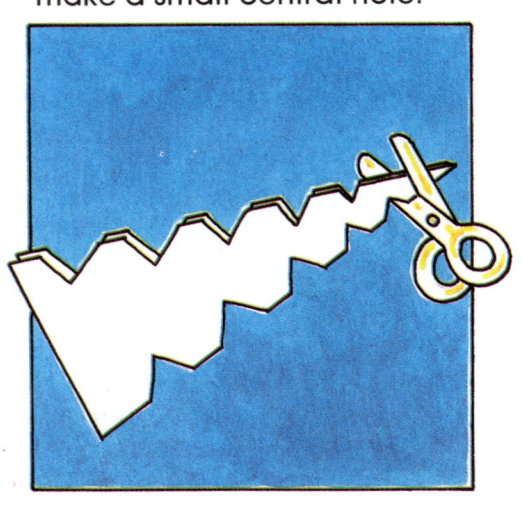

5. Open up the snipped circle and tape into a cone shape.

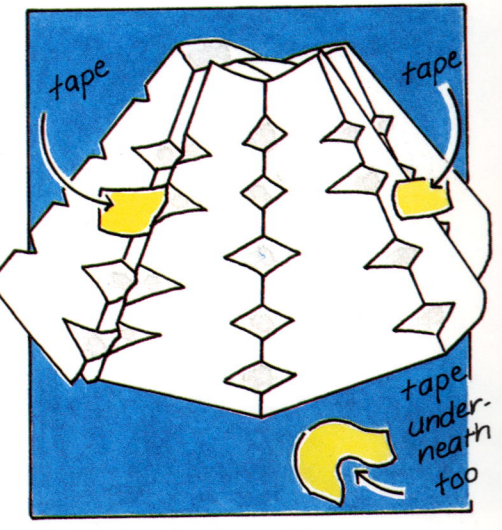

6. Make the head by wrapping some terylene wadding into a piece of old tights and fasten with an elastic band. Push the ends into the hole at the top of the cone and fix in place with tape or by pulling a piece of the elastic band over the paper, too.

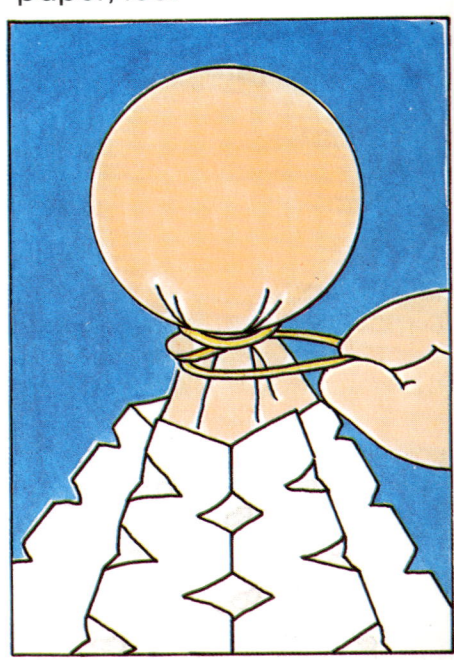

7. Make hair by cutting strands of wool, tying them together, and knotting the bundle to the top of the head. Cut a fringe if you like, then draw on the features with felt pens.

8. Make wings and arms out of the remaining scraps of cut-off paper and stick them on to the body.

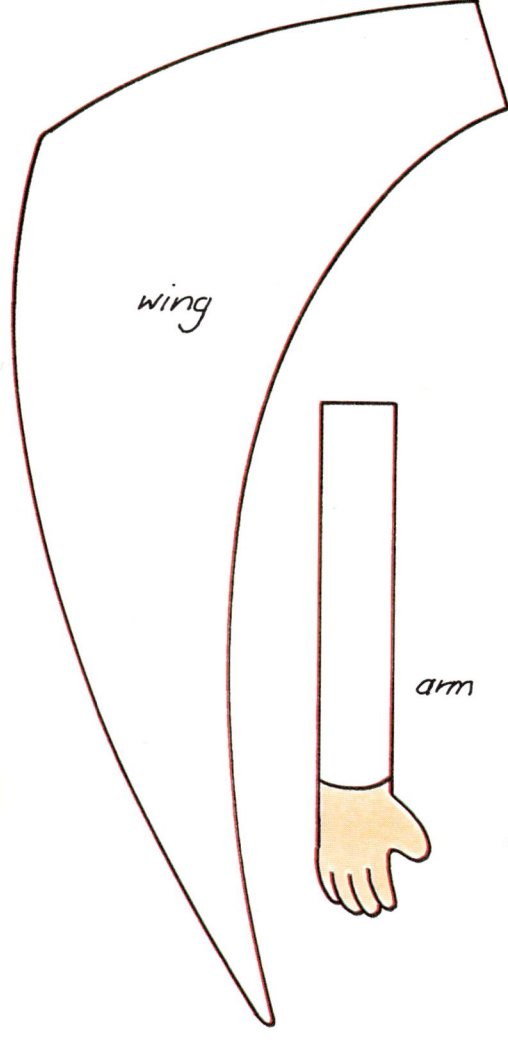

wing

arm

9. Make eight more out of the other sheets of paper.

To make the Manger

1. Make a small box shape out of cardboard, and add four legs, one at each corner, with sticky tape. Use felt pens to make wood markings on the outside.

2. Roll a small piece of terylene wadding in a piece of old tights and wrap it up in the white cloth. Draw on a face and place it among straw in the manger, for the baby.

To Assemble

1. Make two cardboard stars from the star pattern below and cover each one with silver foil. Tape them together over the hook of the coat-hanger.

2. Fix four angels to dangle from the hanger, evenly spaced, on very short threads.

3. Fix three others on longer thread to dangle between them.

4. Fix the last two to threads attached to the hems of the centre two on the top row.

5. Dangle the manger from the hem of each of the bottom two angels.

6. Hang it up with a thread fixed around the centre of the coat-hanger.

Tablecloth and napkins

This isn't something which can be kept from year to year — but don't get upset about throwing it away after the meal — you can do another one next year!

**You'll need:
A plain white paper tablecloth
Plain white paper napkins
Poster or acrylic paints
Stiff, thick brushes
Card
A grown-up with a craft knife, or a sharp pair of small scissors
Masking tape**

1. If you want to do this all by yourself, use the scissors, but don't use the craft knife yourself. If it slips you could have a very unhappy Christmas..

2. Choose one of the stencil patterns opposite and trace it on to card.
Cut out the shapes.

3. Mix up some stiff paint. Place the tablecloth on to your working surface and secure the stencil in place with masking tape — don't use any other kind of tape for this as it could be hard to remove later.

4. Dip a brush in the paint and dab it on to the parts of the tablecloth revealed in the stencil design. You need green for the holly leaves, red for the berries, and yellow for the bell if you use it in the same design. The Christmas tree is green, of course, with a pot and baubles of a different shade. The star should be yellow. The word NOEL may be in any combination of colours which you like.

5. When you have finished the tablecloth repeat the chosen motif on the napkins. You may need to cut another stencil after a while, as the cardboard will wear out.

Stencils

NOËL

Paper hats

Christmas isn't Christmas unless everyone gets to wear a paper hat at least *some* of the time! But the ones you get out of crackers are so boring ... and anyway, if you make your own crackers you'll need separate hats ... so here are some really personal ones.

1. Make triangular hats out of left-over bits of wallpaper. You'll need quite a big piece. Fold it in half, then fold as shown in the diagrams. Staple on personal things like cut-out painted names, remarks (only nice ones, please, even for horrible little brothers and bossy big sisters, because it is the season of goodwill) and things which they might like (cuddly teddies, pictures of cream cakes, cut-outs of darts, knitting, and so on.)

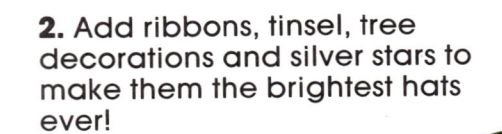

2. Add ribbons, tinsel, tree decorations and silver stars to make them the brightest hats ever!

A tree for the table

This is a pretty centrepiece for Christmas Day! Tasty, too!

You'll need:
Green card — enough to cut out five trees
Silver thread and a needle with an eye big enough to take the thread
After-dinner chocolate mints wrapped in silver foil
Transparent sticky tape

1. Trace the half-tree pattern from the stencil page on to a sheet of folded paper. Then you have your pattern for the Table Tree.

2. Cut out five trees from the pattern (which, remember, is a full tree) from the green card. Fold each one in half.

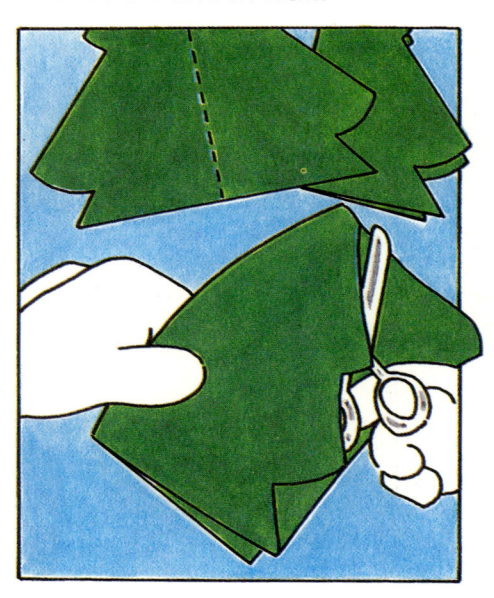

3. Tape silver thread to the mints, tie them at the top, and thread the ends on to the needle.

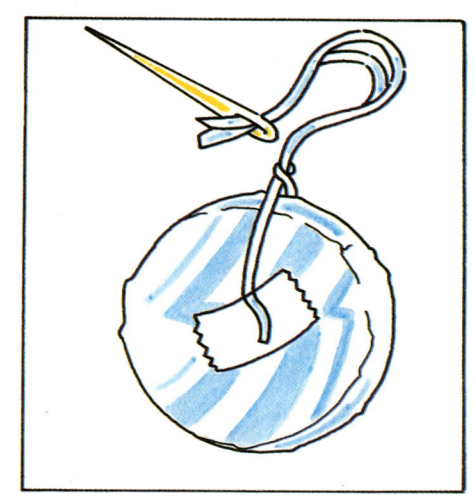

4. Push the needle through the card from the inside of each folded card to the outside so that the mints dangle inside the fold at random intervals, securing each one with sticky tape.

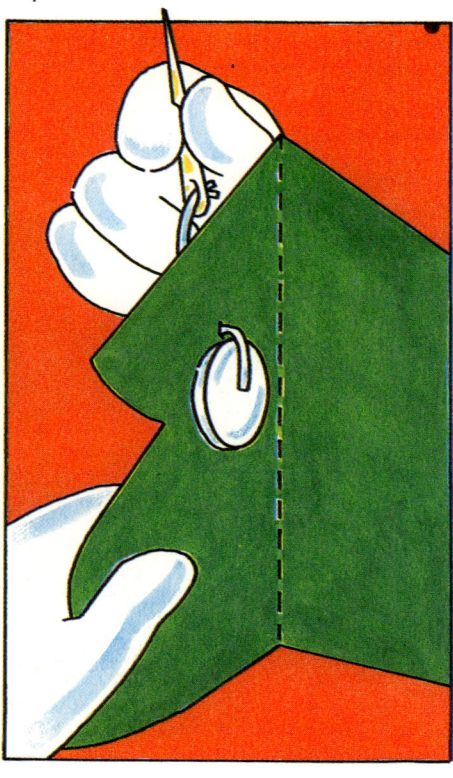

5. Glue the outsides of the cards together to make a five-sided tree. The taped ends of the silver thread will then be hidden and the tree will stand on the table. Trim the edges to match after glueing if necessary.

6. Have a pair of scissors handy to cut the parcels from the tree after the meal.

Tree decorations

Star Turns

You'll need:
An empty plastic pop bottle
Card
Silver foil
Scissors
Glue
Thread
Sticky Tape

1. Cut the pop bottle into rings about 15 mm thick.

2. Make cardboard stars to fit inside these rings and cover them with silver foil.

3. Make tiny holes in the star and rings so that you can thread the stars to hang inside the rings. Add a piece of thread to dangle the whole thing from a tree branch.

Citric Sparklers

You'll need:
Empty plastic lemons
Glue
Glitter and/or sequins
Thread
Pencils

1. Wash out the lemons thoroughly so that they are quite clean.

2. Wedge the pencils into something so that they stand upright, and you can put a lemon on top of each one. Keep the tops of the lemons, so that you can replace them later.

3. Cover each lemon with glue. Put glitter or sequins on to the glue and leave to dry.

4. You could make patterns if you have more than one type of decoration — there could be swirls, or stripes, or lemons which are one colour on one half and another on the other.

Sweet Cones

Fir trees have cones — but not usually like this!

You'll need:
Semi-circles of stiff paper — a good Christmassy design is fine. Draw round a tea plate to get a circle, then cut the circle in half
Sweets
Braid or paper fringing (braid costs money, but you can make the fringing yourself by snipping a strip of paper)
Glue
Thin ribbon

1. Fold the semi-circle into a cone shape and glue together. Glue braid or fringing around the top edge.

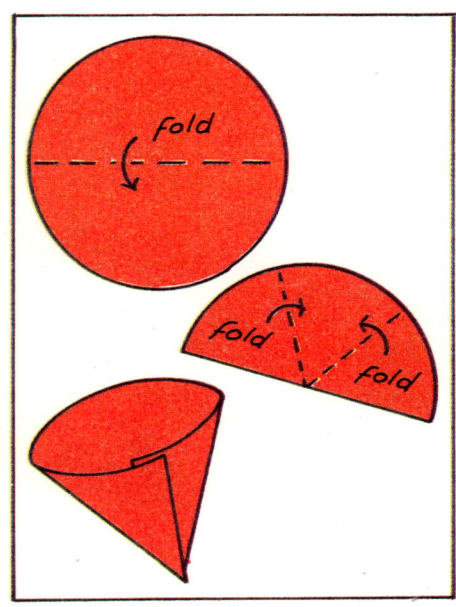

2. Fill with sweets and hang up.

Christmas Stockings

You'll need:
Red card
Small amount of terylene wadding
Thread

1. Cut out lots of little red stockings using the pattern below.

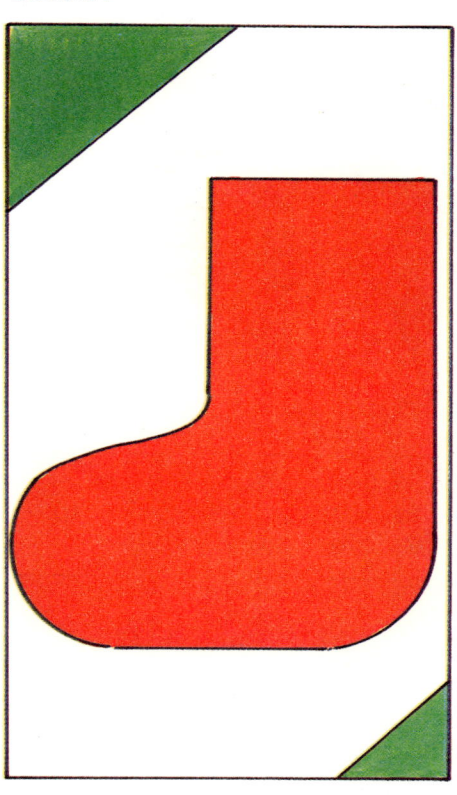

2. Cut thin strips of terylene wadding and glue them to the top of the stockings.

3. Hang them up from the top, using thread.

4. You could make a line of these stockings, each one with a letter of the message HAPPY CHRISTMAS on it, and hang them on the door, or under a picture. You could even join them together and stuff them into an envelope, and give it to someone as an unusual Christmas card.

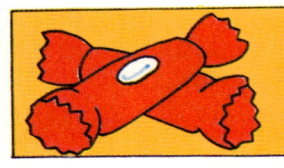

Christmas crackers

You'll need:
For each cracker:
Crepe paper,
180 mm × 320mm (the grain should run lengthwise)
White paper,
160 mm × 300 mm
Piece of thin card,
115 mm × 150 mm
3 empty toilet rolls
Small piece of paper for the joke
Transparent sticky tape
Glue
String
A small present

1. Crackers are also supposed to have snaps inside to make the bang — but these can be hard to find. Never mind if you can't find any to buy — just tell everyone that you have to shout 'Bang' as you pull these crackers and they will be just as noisy as shop-bought ones.

2. Fasten two of the toilet rolls together with tape.

3. Crinkle the short edges of the crepe paper by tweaking them all the way along between finger and thumb.

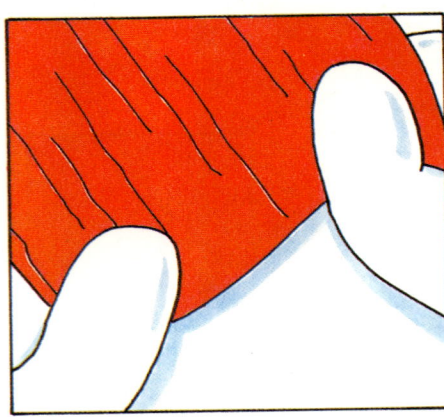

4. Write a joke on the paper and draw a little cartoon to illustrate it too, if you like.

5. Place the white paper centrally on the crepe paper, with the joke and snap (if you have one) on top.

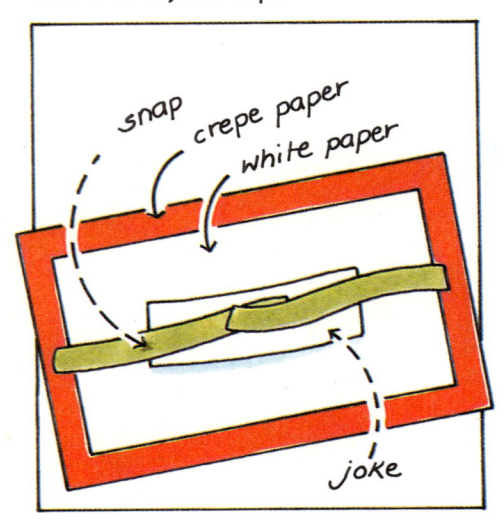

6. Put the thin card over that, with the short edges towards the long edges of the crepe paper. Put glue along one long edge of the crepe paper.

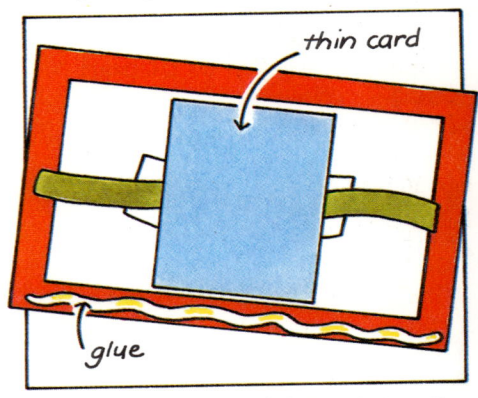

7. Place the double toilet roll on the card so that one end is against the edge of the card.

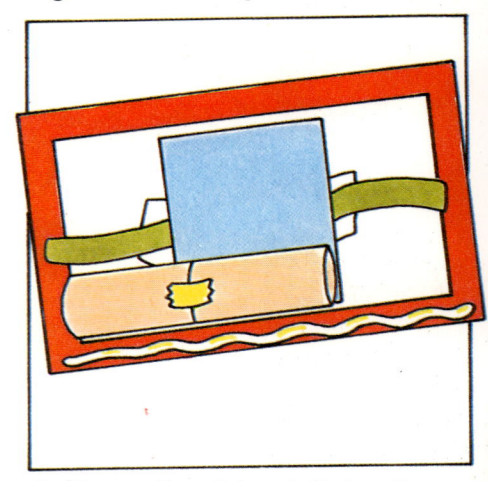

8. Place the third toilet roll next to the others.

9. Wrap the whole thing up tightly and press the glued edge of crepe paper down to secure it.

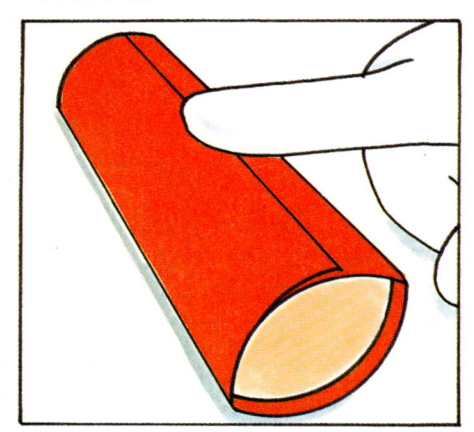

10. When the glue has set, pull the third toilet roll out about 40 mm.

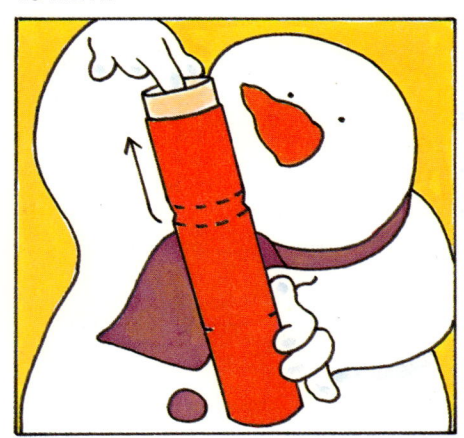

11. Place a piece of string under the gap between rolls which you have just made. Bring the ends up and overlap them. Pull them tight, then remove the string and twist the cracker at this point to make the crease sharper.

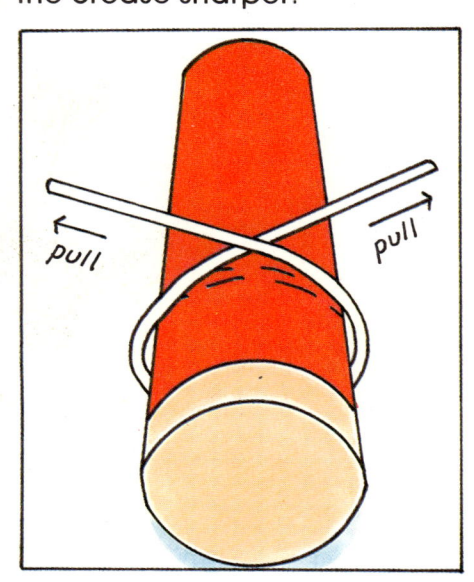

12. Remove the single toilet roll completely, then turn the cracker up the other way and remove the double roll. Pop the gift inside.

13. Insert the single roll into this end now, but don't push it right up to the card in the centre; leave a 40 mm gap as you made at the other end and use the string to begin the crease as before. Then remove the string and twist to form the deep crease.

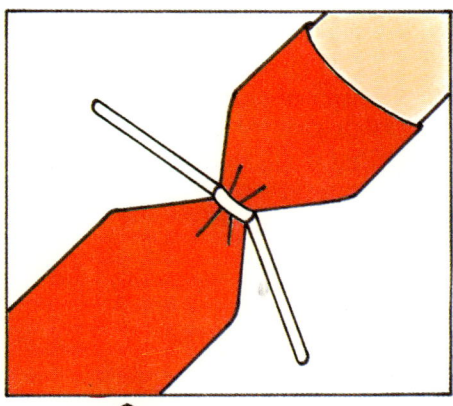

14. Decorating your cracker can make all the difference between a success and a failure. Some craft shops sell sequin waste which makes a lovely sparkly decoration for crackers; it's a strip which has had the sequins punched out of it leaving a shiny kind of lacy ribbon which is stiff enough to hold the shape you make it take, and is great for rosettes on the centre of crackers and added in a tubular way to the ends. You can use lace and immitation flowers, too — or cut-outs from glossy wrapping paper.

15. Tinsel and silver foil on white crepe paper looks spectacular — and if you want something really personal, because you have filled your crackers with certain members of your family in mind, see if you can find a photograph of the people to stick on the front of each one, amid some tinsel and glitter.

Candleholders and trees

These decorations are made of a very salty dough and will last and last through many Christmasses.

You'll need:
8 heaped tablespoons of plain white flour
6 heaped tablespoons of salt
Acrylic or gouache paints
Brushes
Polyurethane varnish
White spirit and washing-up liquid for cleaning the brushes
Candles
For the tree trees only:
An egg and a tablespoon of cold water

1. Mix the salt and flour together very thoroughly and gradually add enough cold water to make a stiff dough. Add more flour if it goes a bit stretchy.

2. Knead it for ten minutes. Kneading means pummelling it about on a floury surface; you should like doing that.

3. To make a candleholder, roll out a piece of dough and cut it into a circle with a large circular pastry cutter, or by placing a glass on top and pressing down.

4. Wet the centre of the circle and press a lump of dough on it. Press a candle into this and then remove it. Push your thumb against the outside of the lump to help it to join on to the base.

5. Cut out holly leaves from rolled-out dough and fix them to the base with water and a few pinches here and there. Add some small rolled balls of dough for berries.

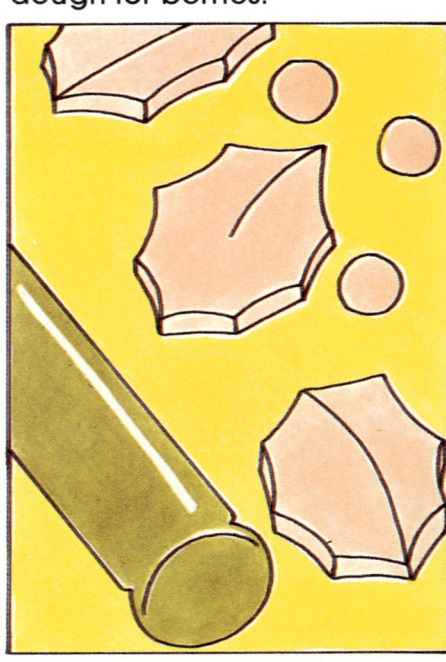

6. Place on a foil dish and cook for about 1½ hours at Gas Mark 1½, 145°C or 290°F.

7. When it has completely cooled, paint it. How about a black base, with red berries and green leaves? Then, when the paint is dry, give it a coat of varnish, and be sure to clean the brushes well afterwards.

8. To make trees, cut triangles which have a little stem on the bottom. Then snip small pieces all over the triangle part with scissors to look like the ends of branches. Bake them as for the candleholder, but before you do, paint them with a glaze made of the beaten egg and water. Poke a tiny hole in the top just before they go into the oven, and renew it when you take them out.

9. Thread narrow red ribbon through these holes for hanging on the tree.

10. EXTRA IDEA: In the section on Christmas wreaths there is a suggestion for a cardboard wreath. You could make the same thing out of dough if you liked.

Wrapping paper and tags

Who needs expensive glossy paper when you can design your own? Well — it's nice to have the bought stuff sometimes, but making your own is fun, and cheap, too.

**You'll need:
Poster or powder paints, nicely mixed to a sticky, sloppy goo
An old toothbrush or two
Pieces of sponge cloth (the washing-up sort)
Scissors
Brushes
Lots of brown paper
Roll of wallpaper lining paper
Plenty of newspaper to protect all surfaces
Overalls to protect *you*
Indoor line to peg up finished paper to dry.**

Cut the lining paper into 75 cm lengths and stack in a corner out of the way, so that it doesn't get covered in paint before it should, or get crumpled. It's best, before you start, to work out where you are going to hang up the paper to dry when you have painted it, or you could end up in a right old mess and your mum could quickly run out of the festive spirit.

Sprayed paper

1. Have some very runny colours ready and dip an old toothbrush into one of them. Spatter it over the paper. Use another toothbrush for another colour — or wash and dry the used one before changing colours.

2. Use this technique on brown paper with white paint, and then paint snowmen every so often on top. On white paper you can just make a colourful mess! Or try spattering paint on top of a paper doily placed over the paper, moving the doily around to get an all-over pattern.

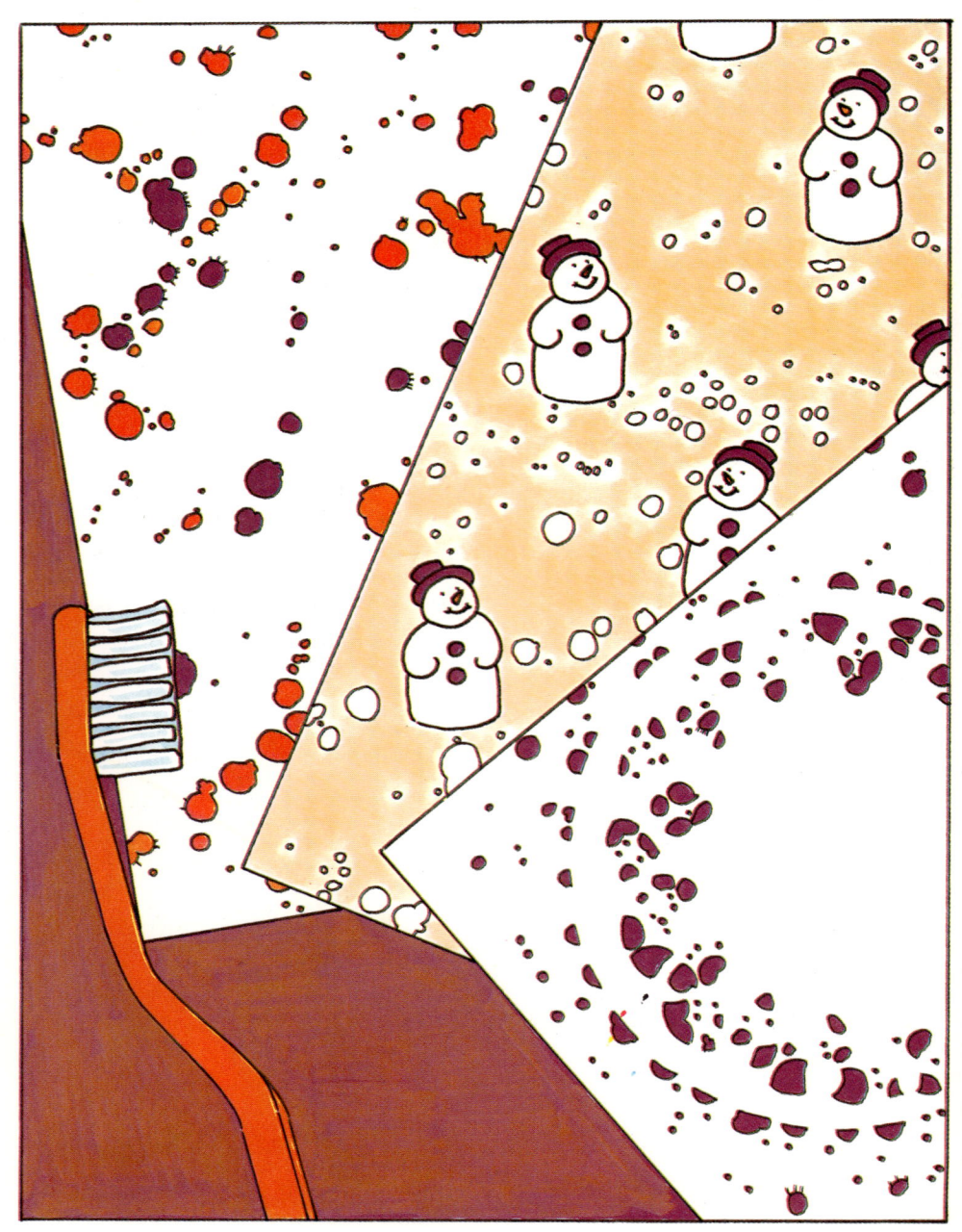

Sponge Designs

Cut designs out of washing-up sponges and dip them into thin layers of paint in a saucer before pressing them down on the paper. You can do Christmas trees, stars and holly leaves quite well like this. Add berries to the holly leaves with red paint blobs, and dots of colour decoration to the trees. The stars can be in different colours.

Finger swirls

You're sure to get it on your hands eventually, so make a point of it and do some finger-painting! Try dragging your green-paint-loaded fingers down a sheet of paper for a garland, and add splodgy thumb-print baubles of other colours. Easy to do and very Christmassy!

Painted Presents

Cut squares of sponge and press them first in the paint and then on the paper. Using a brush, turn them into parcels by painting bows and ribbons on them.

Just Personal

How many different ways are there of writing someone's name? If you know whose present is going to be wrapped in a certain sheet of paper, paint his or her name all over it. But it might be too tempting for that person if it is left under the tree — maybe presents wrapped up like this should be brought out at the last minute!

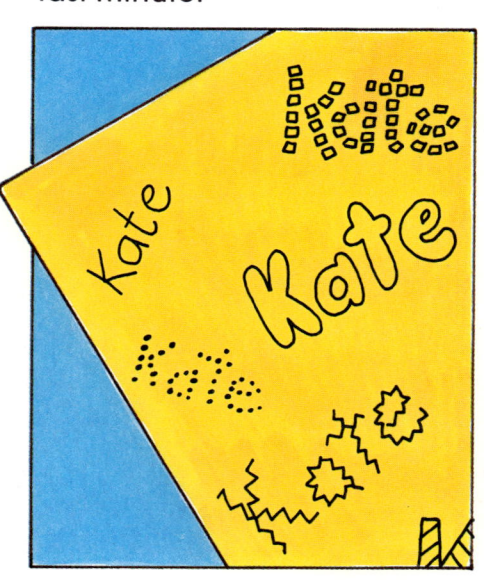

Tags

1. You'll need white card for these. If they are to match brown wrapping paper designs, cut some of the brown wrapping paper to stick on the front of the tag, and paint it in the same way as you did the big piece.

2. Spatter the tags to go with the spattered wrapping paper, and sponge tags all over the outside of the tags if they are to go with sponged wrapping paper designs. Painted Present paper could have tags in the shape of the printed parcels.

3. Just Personal paper could have plain tags — but they should say HAPPY CHRISTMAS inside.

Christmas envelopes

To make a special envelope for a handmade card or flat present, you'll need to spend a little money and time . . . but it will look superb when it's finished!

You'll need:
Christmassy wrapping paper
Lace edging
Fine ribbon

1. Work out how big your finished envelope needs to be. There's nothing worse than finding out afterwards that it needed to be a little bit bigger!

2. Your paper will need to be three times the size of the finished envelope — look at the diagram to see how to mark it out. You'll need a little extra on each long side for glueing, and along one short side to fold over for neatness and strength.

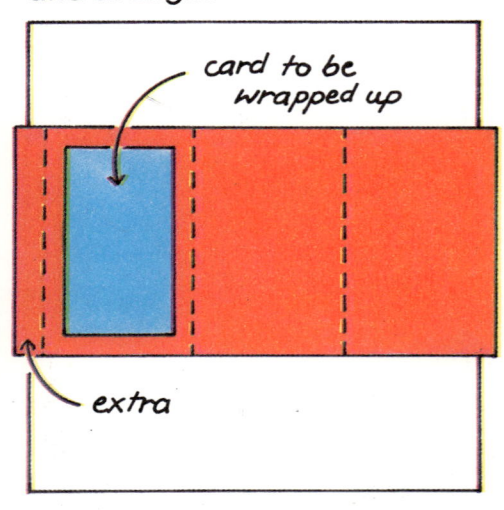

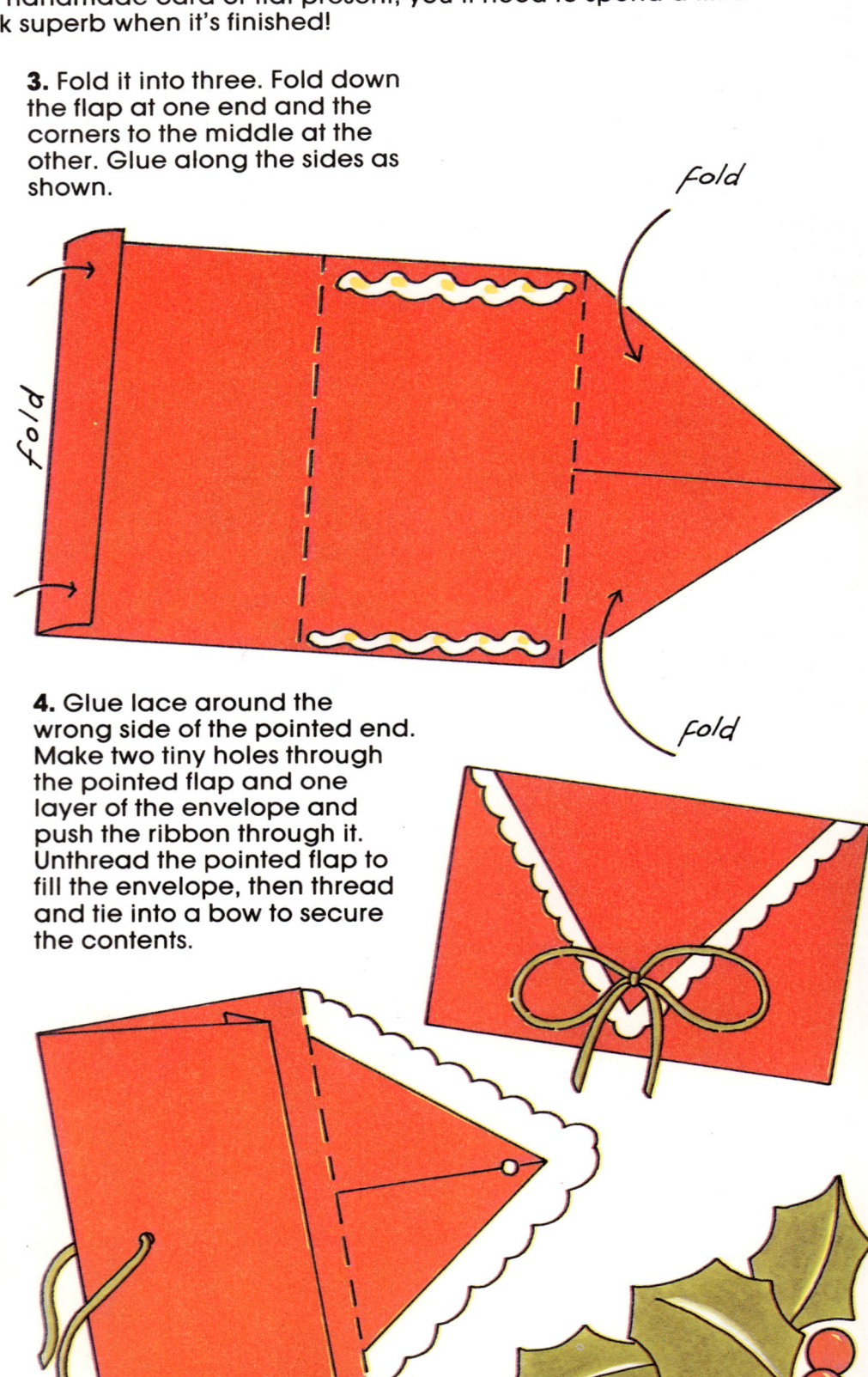

3. Fold it into three. Fold down the flap at one end and the corners to the middle at the other. Glue along the sides as shown.

4. Glue lace around the wrong side of the pointed end. Make two tiny holes through the pointed flap and one layer of the envelope and push the ribbon through it. Unthread the pointed flap to fill the envelope, then thread and tie into a bow to secure the contents.

A nativity scene

Our Nativity figures are no flat cardboard cut-outs — they are solid little figures which you can store through the year and bring out every Christmas.

You'll need:
Individual plastic fizzy drink bottles (about 160 mm high)
Old tights
Terylene wadding
Scraps of fabric, ribbon, braid etc
Silver and gold card
Small amount of brown, black and white wool
Needle, thread and scissors
Trimmings
Sticky tape

1. We've put 'trimmings' because all kinds of things can be used in a Nativity scene; a broken brooch can become a king's diadem, large beads or bottletops will do for gifts of gold, frankincense or myrrh... there is a good case for never throwing anything away when you want to make things like this!

2. A fizzy drink bottle forms the body of each figure except the Baby Jesus. To this must be attached arms and a head. We tried several different kinds of arms; Mary has cardboard ones, painted flesh-coloured on both sides, but everyone else has padded cloth arms. You could make cloth arms for Mary, too, if you liked; just make them thinner than everyone else's, because although it's fine for Joseph, the shepherd, and even the Wise Men to be big and beefy, it's better if Mary is a little more delicate. Should you have one slightly slimmer, shorter pop bottle than the others, this is the one for Mary.

3. Adding the Head
Cut a 60 mm section of tights leg and put some terylene wadding inside. Shape this around the neck of the bottle, tucking the raw end up under the wadding at what is to be the face. Twist the rest round the back of the head and tuck inside the top of the bottle. Pull the top of the face over this and secure with a few stitches at the back of the head. Don't put the face details on yet — it's best to do them last, when you see how much of this has to be covered with a head-dress.

Mary

4. Trace Mary's arm pattern on to white card. Cut out two, reversing one so that she has a left and right arm. Tape these to the top of the bottle, just under the head, when you have coloured them.

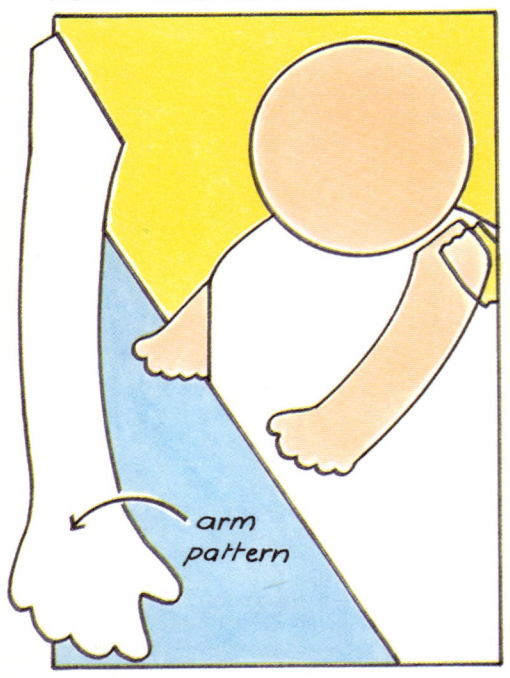

5. Cut a strip of blue fabric about 100 mm × 150 mm and fold the raw edge under along one long side. With this folded edge to the front, wrap it round her head and across her chest, securing to the bottle with sticky tape.

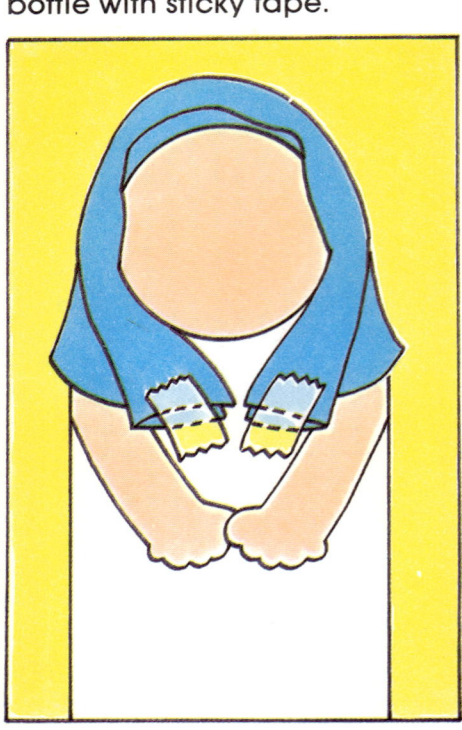

6. Cut another piece of blue fabric big enough to wrap round the bottle and cross over at the front, and long enough to cover the bottle from neck to base. If you like sewing you could hem the bottom of this, but you could also make it a lot longer and fold it up from the hem so that it looks neat without having to sew it. Wrap this round Mary, cutting slits to let the arms through, and tucking in raw edges round the neck. Secure in place round the middle with a bit of ribbon or braid, tied at the back.

7. Pull any bumps and bulges through to the back and make Mary a rectangular shawl, to fix under her chin with a few neat stitches with the rest of it hanging down her back, over the awkward bits. Draw in the eyes and mouth with felt pens.

Baby Jesus

8. Wrap a bit of Terylene wadding in a piece of old tights, and wrap it up in a scrap of white cloth. Place it in Mary's arms, sewing through her fingers to make sure she doesn't drop him. Draw in the face with felt pens.

Joseph

9. Joseph and all the others — kings, shepherds — need arms. To make Joseph's and the shepherds', cut a strip of old tights which is 50 mm × 180 mm. Wrap some terylene wadding in this and stitch into a strip. Embroider the hand details on to the ends if liked, using backstitch down the fingers. Sew this centrally to the back of the head.

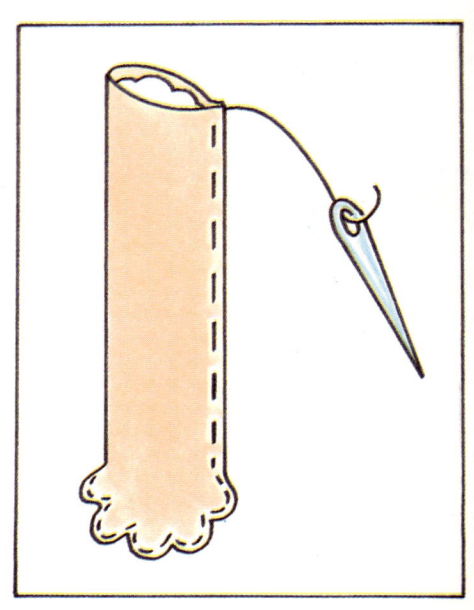

10. Make a tunic for Joseph. To do this, take a piece of fabric which is a little longer than the bottle is tall, and is long enough to wrap round the bottle twice. Find the central point, which will come at the back of the neck. Fold each side a little way past this point so that the fronts overlap. Cut arms as in the diagram, and slope the shoulders. Place right sides together and sew fronts to back, leaving openings for the neck by only sewing shoulders, under-arm and side seams. Turn right side out and dress Joseph in it, securing with a ribbon belt.

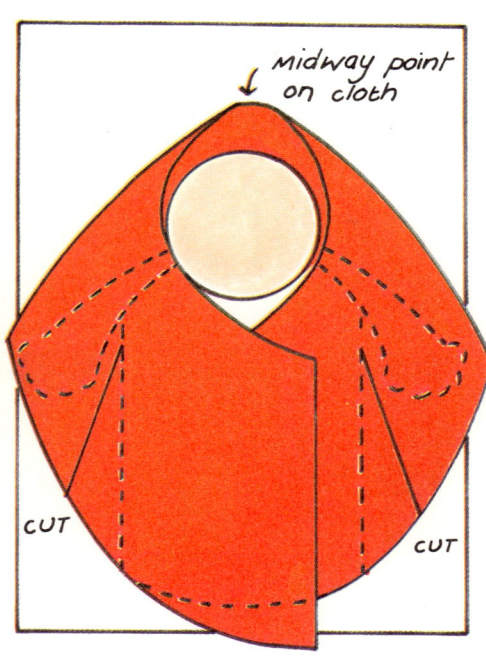

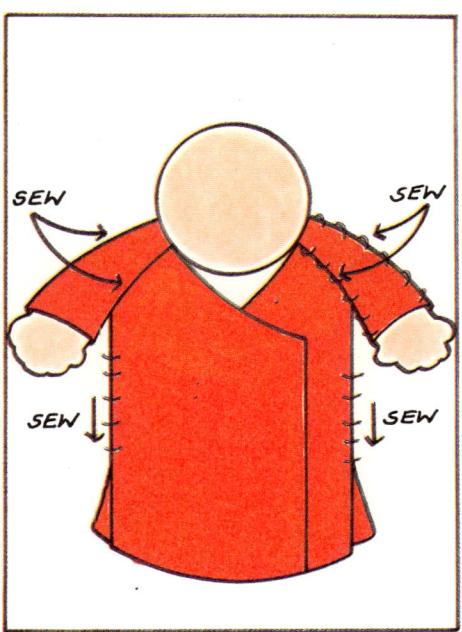

11. Place a square of cloth on his head and sew a piece of narrow braid or felt around it to secure in place. Add the facial details with felt pens. Our Joseph had a bit of a lumpy face so we turned the lumpiness into a beard!

Shepherds

12. Shepherds are made like Joseph, but using different fabric. Dress them in rather more drab cloth than you use for Joseph, and give them little lambs to hold. These can be made from flat shapes of terylene wadding with white thread wrapped round their necks and legs to make them separate from their bodies. Otherwise, use white card and glue cotton wool or terylene wadding to the shapes.

Kings

13. This is where you can use all your richest scraps of fabric, your sequins, bits of old hair slides and so on. We made their arms out of a strip of the fabric used for their clothes, and used the old tights at the ends, stuffed with wadding for hands, tucking the raw ends in. The bottle was covered in the same fabric as used for the arms, put on first with the join at the back, so do yours this way too, and you'll then be able to stitch the arms on to this, making them come round to the front by stitching them round nearly to the front.

14. You can add extra pieces of fabric as skirts, to brighten them up, or make silver foil stars and moons to hang round their hems. Make cloaks for them, because cloaks cover up all the joins at the back just as Mary's head-dress did. To do this, cut a rectangle of velvet or brocade, or something else nice, and fold under about 5 mm at the top. Run a gathering thread along this, pull up tight, and use this thread to stitch the cloak to the neck.

15. You can use black or brown woolly hair, or use scraps of terylene wadding. One of our kings has a beard of this — eyebrows, too. Crowns can be made of foil and sequins stuck to them, or glitter applied on top of glue.

16. If you'd rather put Jesus in the manger instead of letting Mary hold him all through Christmas, make one out of a margarine tub or cardboard carton. Add some strong cardboard legs and paint the sides brown, and fill with straw. If straw is hard to come by, ask at your local glass and china shop for some of the shredded paper strips which they use when wrapping delicate items.

17. Don't forget the kings' gifts!

Sweet gifts

Truffles are everyone's favourite at Christmas. Here are some for you to make and give as presents. Pack them in egg boxes which you have decorated with a bit of tinsel!

You'll need:
150 g plain dark chocolate
25 g butter
100 g shortbread biscuits
1 tablespoon orange juice
1 egg white
¼ teaspoon ground cinnamon
25 g caster sugar
Chocolate vermicelli

1. Crush the biscuits by putting them into a polythene bag and rolling firmly over them with a rolling pin.

2. Break up the chocolate and melt it in a microwave oven in a suitable bowl, or in a heatproof bowl over a pan of hot water on the stove.

3. Stir in the butter and when it has melted add the crushed biscuits and orange juice. Mix it all well together.

4. Form it into small balls, dusting your fingers with icing sugar if it seems sticky.

5. Mix the caster sugar and ground cinnamon in a dish and put some chocolate vermicelli in another. Paint egg white on to each truffle and roll half of them in vermicelli, half in the sugar mixture. Leave to dry for several hours but then pack and give them to a friend with instructions to eat them up within two weeks.

Bet they will!

Sew a Christmas message

You'll need:
Cross-stitch canvas
Red, green and white wool
4 brass curtain rings
Cardboard
Felt for backing

1. Because there are many different types of cross-stitch canvas available we have not given you exact measurements for this design. Ours was worked on a strong plastic grid which didn't need cardboard to stiffen it. But as this could be hard to find you can use any canvas made for cross-stitch work. Just work the design, leaving enough bare canvas around it to fold under at least 5 mm afterwards on each of the three panels.

2. The stitch we used is Half Cross Stitch, because when you are using wool the fibres are thick enough not to let any canvas show between stitches. Look at the diagram to see how this stitch is worked.

3. Following the charts, work three panels. You'll see that you should have 19 stitches in each row, and each panel should be 19 rows deep.

· = Red
/ = White
o = Green

4. Cut three cardboard squares just a little bit smaller than the worked area of the panels. Cut three pieces of backing felt to the exact measurement of the worked part of the panels.

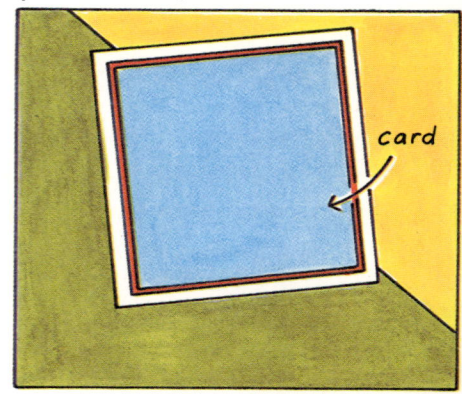

5. Cut the corners of the **J** panel as shown.

6. Fold back the seam allowance of the **J** panel over one of the cardboard squares. Pin a felt square over that so that the edges meet all round with a tiny strip of canvas showing.

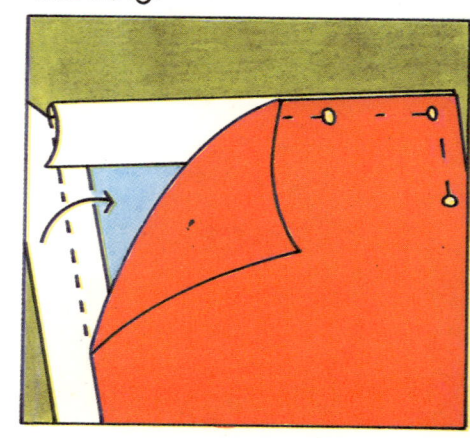

7. Beginning in the top left corner and using Green, work 3 stitches into the corner, going into the same spot each time in the backing felt as well as the canvas. You should not have to stitch through the cardboard as you cut it a little smaller.

8. Work 7 stitches along the top edge, then work the next 5 stitches through a brass curtain ring. Continue to the end, turning the corner with three stitches, all in the same place in the backing felt as for the first corner.

9. Work straight all down the side, turning the corner with 3 stitches as before. Work along the bottom, inserting a brass curtain ring as you did along the top. Turn the last corner with 3 stitches and work straight up to the top. Fasten off and sew in ends.

10. Do the same to the **O** panel, working the top row joining stitches into the ring at the base of the **J** panel, and using a new ring at the base of the **O**.

11. Then add the **Y** panel in the same way.

12. Finish off with a tassel made from strands of Green wool, hanging from the bottom ring.

Twelfth night box

You'll need:
12 matchboxes
Card
Paints or colouring pens
12 brass paper fasteners
12 tiny gifts to put inside the matchboxes
Christmassy wrapping paper, if liked
Glue

1. Stack all the matchboxes on top of each other and glue them together.

2. Cut card to fit all round and cover the sides, the top and the bottom of the matchbox tower.

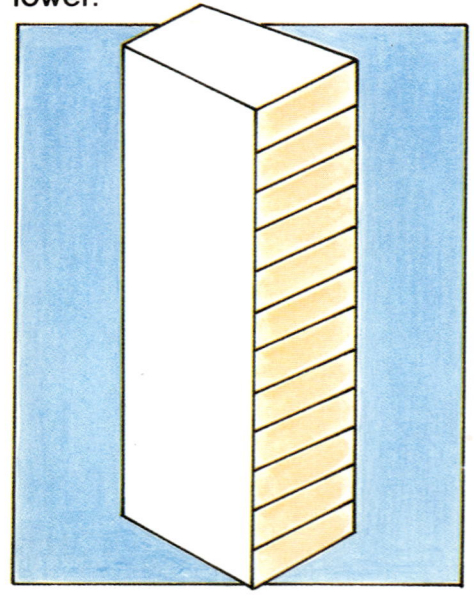

3. Cover this with Christmassy paper, or paint scenes of the 12 days of Christmas on it.

4. Push a brass paper fastener through the front end of each matchbox drawer, as a little knob to open and close it.

5. Paint or write in pen numbers from 1 to 12 on each drawer. It looks better if you write the odd numbers on the left of the knobs and even numbers to the right.

6. Pop the gifts into the drawers. Here are some ideas for gifts:

Day 1 (A partridge in a pear tree) A pear drop — wrap it up first or it will go fluffy!
Day 2 (Two turtle doves) A dove brooch — you could make it out of card, with a safety pin on the back.
Day 3 (Three French hens) How about a little chocolate egg?
Day 4 (Four calling birds) Sounds noisy — can you find a tiny whistle?
Day 5 (Five gold rings) A Christmas cracker ring would be ideal.
Day 6 (Six geese a'laying) A goose from a farmyard set. 
Day 7 (Seven swans a'swimming) A feather!
Day 8 (Eight maids a'milking) A *milk* chocolate miniature.
Day 9 (Nine drummers drumming) A tiny toy drum? Make it out of cardboard if you can't find one.
Day 10 (Ten pipers piping) A tiny trumpet.
Day 11 (Eleven ladies dancing) A doll.
Day 12 (Twelve lords a'leaping) How about a frog?